DATE DUE			

WHEELS
AT WORK AND PLAY

ALL ABOUT
MOTORCYCLES

For a free color catalog describing Gareth Stevens' list of high-quality children's books, call 1-800-341-3569 (USA) or 1-800-461-9120 (Canada).

Wheels at Work and Play
All about Diggers
All about Motorcycles
All about Race Cars
All about Special Engines
All about Tractors
All about Trucks

Library of Congress Cataloging-in-Publication Data

Flint, Russ.
   All about motorcycles / Russ Flint.
      p. cm. — (Wheels at work and play)
   Summary: Depicts a variety of motorcycles and describes the different kinds of races in which they can be driven.
   ISBN 0-8368-0424-4
   1. Motorcycle racing—Juvenile literature. 2. Motorcycles—Juvenile literature. [1. Motorcycles. 2. Motorcycle racing.] I. Title. II. Series.
  GV1060.F58   1990
  796.7'5—dc20
                                               90-9826

This North American library edition first published in 1990 by
Gareth Stevens Children's Books
1555 North RiverCenter Drive, Suite 201
Milwaukee, Wisconsin 53212, USA

First published in North America by
Ideals Publishing Corporation
565 Marriott Drive, Suite 890
Nashville, Tennessee 37210

Series editor: Tom Barnett
Designer: Laurie Shock

Printed in the United States of America

1 2 3 4 5 6 7 8 9 96 95 94 93 92 91 90

WHEELS
AT WORK AND PLAY

ALL ABOUT
MOTORCYCLES

Russ Flint

Gareth Stevens Children's Books
MILWAUKEE

Road-racing bikes
are big. They are fast.

Racers dress to be safe.

A drag race has a
straight track.

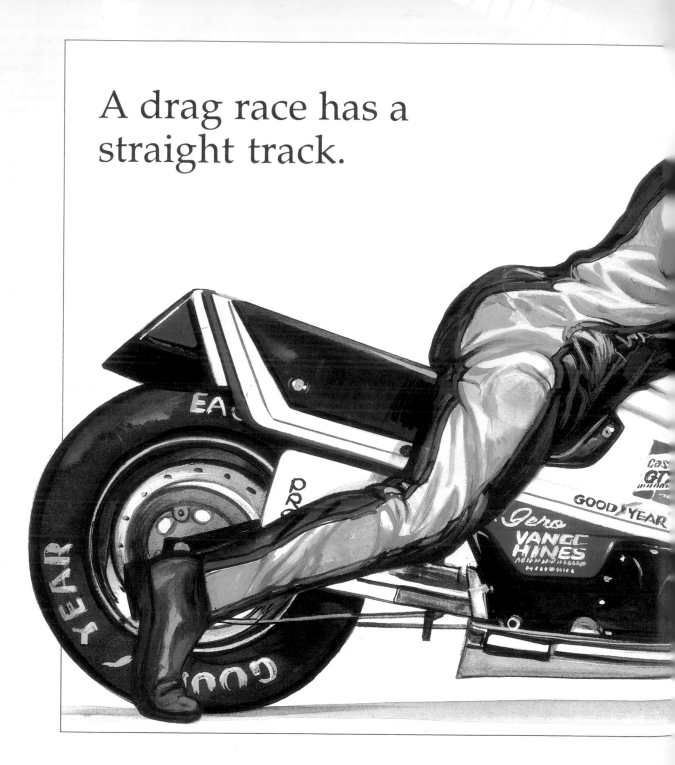

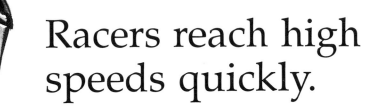

Racers reach high speeds quickly.

Dirt-track racers use their feet on curves.

The speedway racer slides
the bike on curves.

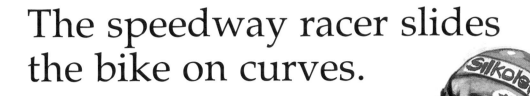

Motocross tracks
are bumpy. They
have many
curves.

The winner
must keep his
wheels on the
ground.

Sidecar racers have
two riders.

Trial riders
must ride
over rocks
and fallen
trees.

Ice-racing bikes don't slip or slide.

Their wheels
dig into the ice.

Glossary

curve
A turn in the road.

dirt-track racers
People who race motorcycles on a curved track covered with dirt.

drag race
A motorcycle race that is held on a straight track.

ice racing
Motorcycle racing that is held on ice-covered tracks. The motor-cycles' wheels have sharp screws in them to dig into the ice.

motocross races
Motorcycle races that are held on a muddy track with many curves and bumps.

road racing
Motorcycle racing that is held on a smooth, curved track.

Index